BELGIUM IN WAR

Termonde as it is to-day

BELGIUM IN WAR

A RECORD OF PERSONAL
EXPERIENCES

BY

J. H. WHITEHOUSE, M.P.

Cambridge :
at the University Press
1915

CAMBRIDGE
UNIVERSITY PRESS

University Printing House, Cambridge CB2 8BS, United Kingdom

Cambridge University Press is part of the University of Cambridge.

It furthers the University's mission by disseminating knowledge in the pursuit of education, learning and research at the highest international levels of excellence.

www.cambridge.org
Information on this title: www.cambridge.org/9781316633267

© Cambridge University Press 1915

First published 1915
First paperback edition 2016

A catalogue record for this publication is available from the British Library

ISBN 978-1-316-63326-7 Paperback

TO
DORRIE
THE COMPANION
OF MY JOURNEY
THIS TRIBUTE OF AFFECTION

INTRODUCTION

BY THE

CHANCELLOR OF THE EXCHEQUER

I AM glad that my friend Mr J. H. White-house, M.P., has allowed the story of his experiences in Belgium during the war to be re-printed in aid of the Relief Funds.

It is a record which enables the reader to realize in part what the war has meant for Belgium, for her children and women and old people, as well as for her soldiers.

I hope its publication may still further extend the welcome which it is the privilege of the British Nation to offer to this brave and much-wronged people.

D. LLOYD GEORGE.

30 *December* 1914.

NOTE

I HAVE to acknowledge the courtesy of the editor of the *Nineteenth Century* in allowing me to reprint much of the matter which appears in this book.

J. H. W.

1 *January* 1915.

CONTENTS

ILLUSTRATIONS

BELGIUM IN WAR

A RECORD OF PERSONAL EXPERIENCES

In September[1] last, whilst the guns of an alien enemy were still sending their messengers of death and destruction, I came to a square in what had been a beautiful town. A few days before this square, and, indeed, the town, too, had been dominated by a noble Gothic church, a legacy from the Middle Ages, the joy and pride of those who had known it. All that remained was the end wall, and only a fragment of that, shot-riddled and tottering. But over what had been the doorway there remained in its original position, undamaged, a figure of the Holy Virgin, holding in her arms the Holy Child. The Child looked upon a scene as horrible as the world has any record of. The Prince of Peace gazed upon a city entirely destroyed. A few hours before it had sheltered thousands of happy human beings. It had embraced many hundreds of peaceful homes. Not one remained. Death and desolation now had sole possession.

[1] 1914.

W. B. W.

1

It is to be doubted whether, even yet, the tragedy of Belgium, with the infinite suffering involved for some millions of non-combatants, has been realised by the world. What has happened? A country containing a population of eight millions of peaceful and industrious persons has suddenly found itself the centre of a conflict between mighty armies, and has been overrun, devastated and ruined. Her life as a nation is destroyed, her people are fugitives, dependent upon the hospitality of the stranger.

The pages of history scarcely offer any parallel for this tragedy in its suddenness, its immensity, and its sacrifice of human life and material wealth.

I visited Belgium with the object of ascertaining the condition of the civilian population generally and of informing myself at first hand as to the conditions set up by the War in an innocent and peaceful country.

I have ever believed that war is the negation of all that is good, and I was anxious to see what its ravages were, and how best its wounds could be healed. But I was not prepared for the reality.

I want to attempt to bring home to my readers what has happened, and this not to arouse passion, but to kindle sympathy.

I reached Antwerp towards the end of September. The King and his Cabinet, with the rest of the members of the Government, exiled from their capital, had made the city their head-quarters and were conducting the work of government as best they could over a sadly shrunken area, Antwerp and

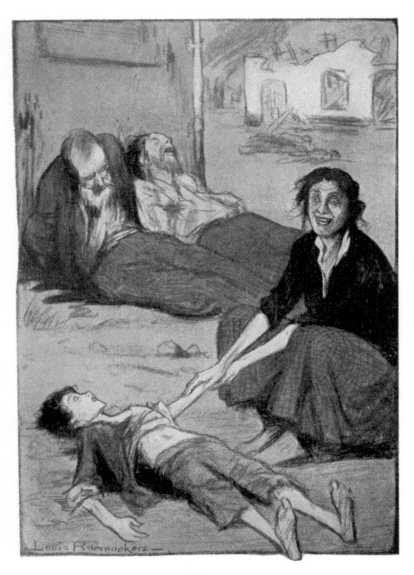

War

"SO EIN FRISCHER FRÖLICHER KRIEG"

Ostend, with the intervening coast line, being practically all that remained to them.

It was thus difficult to get about the country, and, indeed, only possible at all because the Germans frequently withdrew for a time from places they had occupied or destroyed.

On Sunday, the 27th of September, I was received by the King of the Belgians. At the end of the conference I was asked by the King to transmit once more the expression of his thanks for all that was being done for his people by the British nation.

THE CONDITION OF ANTWERP

Antwerp itself, though practically isolated, did not at first glance show many signs of the War then rolling almost to its gates. There were some changes in its physical appearance. The German shops were untenanted and barred. The public buildings, and many private ones, were decorated with the national flag. The streets were crowded, especially in the afternoons and early evenings. Everywhere eager crowds read war telegrams exhibited in shop windows. The Flemish and French papers were bought in large numbers. They contained surprisingly little news, practically nothing of current operations being printed. A large part of the contents of all the papers consisted of reprints from English newspapers three or four days old, or even more. Mr Lloyd George's Queen's Hall speech was being printed and discussed nearly a week after it had been delivered.

Many of the foreign legations had removed to Antwerp with the Government, and were quartered in various hotels in the city.

There was no lack of food within Antwerp. The supplies from Holland had not been interrupted, and the prices of foodstuffs remained normal. It was a noticeable feature at the daily vegetable markets that many very tiny children were acting as food buyers for the homes.

As the city was known to be in danger of attack, refugees from the ravaged districts around were not admitted indiscriminately, but, except in the case of those who came to embark on the English steamers, were sent on to other places and otherwise arranged for.

The possible fate of the wonderful fourteenth-century cathedral, one of the most beautiful Gothic churches in the world, must have been frequently in the minds not only of those who have the guardianship of this world treasure, but of all who know it. Steps were taken for its safety. It displayed from the summit of its incomparable tower a protecting flag. The pictures which usually decorate the interior, including Rubens' famous masterpiece, *The Descent from the Cross*, were removed to the cellars.

One visit which I paid to the cathedral brought home with dramatic force the sacrifice which Belgium was making. It was the hour of the afternoon service. Outside was the crowded eager life of an excited populace, finding outlet for its emotion and solace for its fears in communal intercourse. Inside, the vast congregation was composed largely of women, nearly all of them in deep mourning. Many of them seemed very old; they wept for sons, the little ones clinging to their dress for fathers. Their faces, beautiful with the toil and thought of years, were singularly impressive. They might have stepped from the wonderful Flemish canvases in the Art Gallery of their city.

A few days later these mourning women, old and young, bearing in primitive bundles all that they could save of their household goods, formed part of the procession from the city of its entire population. History itself can scarcely offer a parallel to a spectacle so charged with human suffering. Five hundred thousand peaceful and unoffending inhabitants, homeless and helpless, were fleeing into the darkness. From the banks of the Scheldt amidst flashes of fire they had what for many of them was their last vision of the city of their birth.

At night Antwerp was both dark and silent during the days preceding the bombardment. The shops and cafés closed early. By eight o'clock not a light was to be seen, and the silence was only broken from time to time by the throb of military cars passing through the city.

The German army sent several Zeppelins over Antwerp. The first bomb which was thrown did considerable damage, and killed more than a dozen persons. A married couple who were in the ground-floor room of a house near which the bomb exploded were blown to pieces, and the room presented a very horrible appearance. The Zeppelin raid did not, however, create any general panic, though the city appeared to have no defence against them. A hostile aeroplane came over us at a great height, and the guns which were turned upon it seemed hopelessly inadequate. It did not, however, succeed in doing any damage.

THE DEFENCES OF ANTWERP

In view of subsequent events, it may not be without interest to record what was seen of the defences of Antwerp. It had the reputation of being one of the strongest fortresses in Europe, and had long been intended to serve as the base of the army, should it be compelled to retire in case of the violation of the neutrality of the country. Three circles of forts defended the city. Some of these were built fifty years ago, and all of them before anything was known of the new German siege guns, throwing a shell nearly a ton in weight, for a distance of seven miles, and it was clear to the military authorities that their forts would not stand for long a bombardment under the new conditions, and that additional measures were essential. I was shown

The Flight from Antwerp

what these latter were, and there is no longer any reason for silence respecting them. A bridge of boats had been thrown over the Scheldt west of the city, which served as the chief means of communication with the south-west portion of Belgium. For some miles around Antwerp everything that would afford cover for the Germans was, as far as possible, destroyed. Many thousands of trees were cut down, and their trunks removed or burnt, so that woods and little forests had become barren plains. A large number of houses had been similarly destroyed, and the *débris* carted away or scattered. All the way to the outer line of forts, and beyond, an enormous number of trenches had been prepared. At many strategic points extensive wire entanglements had been prepared, which were electrified and would cause death to any coming into contact with them. I was informed by the Minister of Finance that the value of the property, the destruction of which was rendered necessary by these precautionary measures for the defence of Antwerp amounted to nearly 10,000,000*l*.

The defence guns of Antwerp did not compare with the German siege guns, and the Belgians were further handicapped by some shortage of ammunition, due in part to the fact that some of their ammunition factories were in the hands of the Germans.

THE BELGIAN MINISTRY

The members of the Belgian Government set an example of great bravery and resourcefulness. Each Minister in Antwerp was working incessantly to discharge the duties of government under unexampled conditions of difficulty and danger. They had made arrangements by which they were kept in touch with events in almost every part of the country occupied by the Germans, and they were able to take steps accordingly from day to day, as the situation demanded. There was no panic, or alarm, or excitement in their methods. They were quiet, unassuming men whose lives had hitherto been spent in the paths of peace, but they showed the most unbounded courage. They felt no doubt as to the future, and they made their plans for it in this spirit. Their moderation was very impressive. They distinguished between the German nation and the German army, and realised that there were two Germanys, one which they had known and trusted, and another which was ravaging their land.

The Belgian Ministry gave me every possible assistance in connexion with my mission. Their anxiety throughout was to enable me to see for myself the state of their country. This was a matter of great difficulty, as the German troops were moving rapidly over many parts of the country, and it was not possible to tell a day in advance which points we could attempt to visit.

The Ministry expressed to me their great gratitude for the relief which was coming from England, but they stated that so extensive were the conditions of want and actual starvation that the help they were receiving was as a drop in the ocean. They stated that a great proportion of the population in Belgium were starving, and they gave me the following list of goods as being those most urgently required:

Coal	Flour
Rice	Sugar
Salt	Dry vegetables
Beans	Clothing of all descriptions

They suggested that these articles should be sent direct to Antwerp and that they should undertake their distribution. The German troops were constantly moving and the Government could, therefore, reach a considerable number of the districts most in need. They added that no quantities which the imagination could suggest would be too great to send.

When this conversation took place it was not thought that the Germans would attempt to capture Antwerp. The development of the military situation and the enforced flight of the Government upset, for the time, all the relief schemes. The whole problem has assumed a new character owing to the wholesale exodus of the population from many parts of Belgium.

THE HOSPITALS

Antwerp was, of course, the main and, latterly, the only hospital base for the whole of Belgium. Many of the public buildings had been transformed and were used as emergency hospitals. The hospitals sent by other countries were located here.

I visited most of these hospitals and was impressed by their efficiency. At the outbreak of the war there had been a shortage of surgical requirements, including a notable absence of anaesthetics, but this had since been made good.

No more striking proof of what the war meant to the Belgian nation was needed than a visit to the great military hospital in Antwerp. I hope I may be forgiven for giving a very brief account of my own visit to it. I do not wish to gratify the curiosity of the morbid but to enlist sympathy and aid.

The enormous buildings of the military hospital were filled with the wounded. They included every class of injury. Many were suffering from rifle wounds. These were the least serious cases. The wounds were generally clean, and healed quickly. There were, however, a great number of cases of shell wounds. Some of these were of a very fearful character. The surgeons were working under great pressure. In one operating room the surgeons were dealing with a smashed thigh, caused by shell; in the room adjoining and in the passage connecting, seriously wounded soldiers lay on stretchers waiting to be brought into the operating room.

One portion of the hospital was devoted to wounded Germans. The arrangements for these were the same as for the Belgians. Except that there were armed sentries at the doors there was no distinction. Many of the wounds were serious. One German whom I saw had had both eyes blown out, and was slowly recovering.

I should like to pay a tribute to the devotion of the staff of the British Field Hospital. The school in which it had been placed was filled with Belgians, all seriously wounded. Many of the injuries were from shells and involved complicated and difficult operations. When I was in the hospital I saw an operation being performed on a soldier whose leg had been broken in seventeen places; not only was there a practical certainty of saving the patient's life, but it was also hoped to save the injured limb. This case was typical of many more.

The needs of the Belgian Red Cross Society were brought to my notice. Their funds were exhausted and they were urgently appealing to the Government, already bearing burdens beyond their strength, for immediate financial help. This matter has been brought formally to the notice of the British Red Cross Society, and I trust some of the funds of the latter may be used in Belgium. I believe that public opinion would be wholly in favour of this being done.

TERMONDE

On Saturday, the 26th of September, I was told by the Minister of Finance that it would be possible for me to reach Termonde. Two military motor cars were placed at my disposal. The party with me included the King's Private Secretary and a staff officer. We left Antwerp at midday, and we were enabled to see for ourselves the damage which the Belgians had had to inflict upon themselves in order to protect their city. The destruction of property of every description and the flooding of vast areas of low-lying land gave the appearance of horrible desolation.

When we had gone a little distance we became aware that an attack was being made by the enemy in the neighbourhood of Termonde, and faint echoes of the guns reached us.

We passed through the villages and small towns which cluster round Antwerp, the road being frequently crowded with troops and with innumerable transport waggons going to or returning from the Front. In the villages all ordinary life was arrested, the women and children standing or sitting, dumb and patient, by the roadside. Half way to Termonde we could hear very plainly the booming of the guns. We were hindered in our journey by the destruction of bridges and to some extent by the flooded nature of the country. When, at length, we reached the Scheldt before Termonde, we found a very rough narrow bridge which, with care, we were able to cross. Here the firing was very vivid. There were considerable numbers of Belgian troops, and we saw many evidences of the battle which was then raging. We came to the margin of the town and began our detailed inspection.

I had read newspaper accounts of the destruction of Termonde, and I had seen photographs of houses or parts of streets showing the work of destruction. They had not conveyed to my mind any realisation of the horror of what had actually happened.

Termonde a few weeks ago was a beautiful city of about 16,000 inhabitants; a city in which the dignity of its buildings harmonised with the natural beauty of its situation; a city which contained some buildings of surpassing interest. I found it entirely destroyed; I went through street after street, square after square, and I found that every house was entirely destroyed with all its contents. It was not the result of a bombardment: it was systematic destruction. In each house a separate bomb had been placed which had blown up the interior and had set fire to the contents. All that remained were portions of the outer walls, still constantly falling, and inside the cinders of the contents. Not a shred of furniture or of anything else remained.

This sight continued in street after street throughout the entire extent of what had been a considerable town. It had an indescribable influence upon the observer which no printed description or even pictorial record could give. This influence was increased by the utter silence of the city, broken only by the sound of the guns. Of the population I thought not a soul remained—I was wrong. For as we turned into a square where the wreck of what had been one of the most beautiful of Gothic churches met my eyes, a blind woman and her daughter groped among the ruins. They were the sole living creatures in the whole of the town. Shops, factories, churches, the houses of the wealthy, all were similarly destroyed. One qualification only have I to make of this statement. Two or perhaps three houses bore a German command in chalk that they were not to be burnt. These remained standing, but deserted, amidst the ruins on either side. Where a destroyed house had obviously contained articles of value looting had taken place. In the ruins of what had been a jeweller's shop the remains of the safe were visible amidst the cinders. The part around the lock had been blown off and the contents rifled.

I inquired what had become of the population. It was a question to which no direct reply could be given. They had fled in all directions. Some had reached Antwerp, but a great number were wandering about the country panic-stricken and starving; many were already dead.

A Church at Termonde

THE GENERAL SITUATION THROUGHOUT BELGIUM

I had other opportunities of seeing that what had happened at Termonde was typical of what had happened in other parts of Belgium under the military occupation of Germany, and I have given this record of the condition of Termonde because it is typical.

Conditions of unexampled misery have been set up for the civilian population throughout the occupied territory. Until the fall of Antwerp comparatively only a few refugees had reached this country. The others remained wandering about Belgium flocking into other towns and villages or flying to points a little way across the Dutch frontier. Sometimes when a town has been bombarded the Germans have withdrawn and the civilians have returned to their homes, only to flee again at a renewed attack from the enemy. A case in point is Malines, which on the 27th of September, as I was trying to reach it, was again bombarded. The inhabitants were then unable to leave, as the town was surrounded. But when the bombardment ceased there was a panic exodus.

The whole life of the nation has been arrested; the food supplies which would ordinarily reach the civilian population are being taken by the German troops for their own support. The poor and many others are without the necessaries of life, and the conditions of starvation grow more acute every day. Even where, as in some cases happens, there is a supply of wheat available, the peasants are not allowed to use their windmills owing to the German fear that they will send signals to the Belgian army.

We are face to face with a fact unique perhaps in the history of the world. The life of an entire nation has been arrested, its army is driven to the borders of another country, the bulk of its civilian population are refugees, of those who remain many are panic-stricken wanderers from village to village.

THE GERMAN METHODS IN BELGIUM

As I have already stated, the completeness of the destruction at Termonde was a feature which almost everywhere marked the German progress through Belgium. It was amazing because it was not the result of the ordinary incidents of war such as bombardment. It was organised and systematic destruction. The method of it was explained to me in detail by the Belgian Government, and particularly by the venerable Speaker of the Belgian Parliament. I had explained to me and was shown the numerous appliances which the German soldiers carried for destroying property. Not only were hand-bombs of various sizes and descriptions carried, but each soldier was supplied with a quantity of small black discs little bigger than a sixpenny-piece. I saw these discs which had been taken from German soldiers on

The Retreat from Brussels

the field of battle. These were described to me as being composed of compressed benzine; when lighted they burn brilliantly for a few minutes, and are sufficient to start whatever fire is necessary after the explosion of the bomb.

Many of the German soldiers who were captured were found to be carrying handcuffs, which had apparently been served out to some regiments as a matter of course.

The Belgian Government thought that the object of the German methods was to terrorise the nation, and that their comparative moderation at Brussels was due to the presence of the Ambassadors of neutral countries. I was given instances of the atrocities which the German army was everywhere committing. They were murdering the civil population and they had put to death a large number of priests. The things came as the greater shock to the Government because in 1870 the Germans had observed international laws of war, and their campaign was free from their present cruelties and outrages.

I had described to me by a leading citizen of Liège the incidents following the occupation of that city. He is a distinguished scholar of unimpeachable character. I only refrain from mentioning his name in order not to endanger his safety. He was in Liège throughout the assault and witnessed the arrival of the German troops in the city. From the windows of his own house, saved from destruction by chance because it was next to one occupied by a

German officer, he saw soldiers going from house to house setting each on fire. The terrified occupants rushed from the burning houses, the women and children generally clinging to the men. Again and again he saw the soldiers pull off the women and children, and then shoot the men before their eyes. He witnessed, too, the shooting of a number of priests.

I made myself acquainted with the methods which were being followed by the Commission appointed by the Belgian Government to investigate the methods of the German army. It is a distinguished Commission and it has sifted all its evidence with judicial impartiality. Where witnesses' or even victims' names are suppressed, it is in order to secure the safety of them or their relatives. Their statements are all capable of proof and will bear the strictest investigation. But indeed to one who has seen the ravage of Belgium no other confirmation is necessary.

TACTICS AT LIÈGE AND NAMUR

The Belgian Government described to me the difference in the German methods of attack at Liège and Namur. They explained to me the rushing tactics of great bodies of massed troops at the former place, which resulted in enormous German losses. At Namur these methods were entirely altered. The Germans waited for five days before attacking Namur, and did so only when their siege guns were in position. They relied wholly on these, and the forts of Namur were powerless against them.

A typical scene on the steps of destroyed houses

THE BEGINNING OF THE ATTACK
ON ANTWERP

Reference has already been made to an engagement near Termonde. It was the beginning of the attack which culminated in the evacuation of Antwerp and the flight of the population.

After I had concluded my inspection of the destroyed town I was taken to the south of Termonde, and was made acquainted by the military authorities with the nature of the fighting which was taking place. The enemy were attempting to reoccupy the Termonde district, and, as the next day showed, an advance on Malines, east of Termonde, was part of the same movement.

I was taken as far as the Belgian trenches. Behind me the guns of the protecting forts were thundering. The Belgian soldiers were lying flat in the trenches, which, to a lay mind, appeared to be of a curious formation. They were not cut deep, but a bank was raised on the firing side only, consisting not only of soil, but of wood logs and other miscellaneous things. There was also a rough cover of what appeared to be iron sheets weighted with wood logs and supported by rough stakes—generally small tree trunks. Though this method of trenching might afford some shelter against shells breaking in front of the soldiers, it did not appear to be effective against those breaking behind but near enough for the effect of the explosion to reach the trench.

We could hear the German fire but could see nothing of the enemy. One of his shells came over us, falling well in our rear. Some of the shells fell in the ruined town behind us.

The German attack was successfully resisted on this day and the Belgians held their ground, the enemy by nightfall having retreated about three miles.

We could see in actual working the arrangements for dealing with the wounded on the field of battle. In the rear of the fighting line there waited ambulance men with stretcher-beds. They received the wounded from the Red Cross parties who brought them direct from the trenches. Simple first aid was given and they were then taken to the railway station, happily close at hand, and put into a hospital train in waiting. At Antwerp station conveyances were waiting to take them to the hospitals. These arrangements were carried out as expeditiously as possible, and everything humanly possible was done for the sufferers. But I came to the conclusion that much suffering, and perhaps loss of life, would be avoided if the wounded could be more frequently taken straight to the hospital base by a motor ambulance so as to save the changes and delays with the consequent suffering which transit by train meant. This is in no sense intended as a criticism of the Belgian arrangements, which were the subject of great care and devotion and were as good as was possible.

THE BELGIAN PRIEST IN WAR

Many opportunities occurred to witness the work of the Belgian priests. Of their courage and devotion it would be impossible to speak too highly. In every village they were to be found comforting and helping. In many cases they acted as Red Cross workers and carried the wounded from the battlefield. I saw in the district of the fighting many of these priests waiting by the side of their stretchers. They retained their long black dress, the only difference they had made being the assumption of the Red Cross band on their arms.

Their work in this connexion should be remembered in view of the considerable numbers who have been put to death by the Germans. I remember, too, with gratitude and admiration the vision I had of their work when I returned to England in a boat crowded with refugees. They moved about the great crowd huddled together during a violent storm, doing all they could to relieve the sufferings of those poor beings already panic-stricken by their experiences on land, to which was now added the horror of a storm at sea as they journeyed to an unknown land.

SUMMARY OF THE PRESENT POSITION

To attempt to sum up, Belgium has suffered destruction in the following different ways, each of them almost equally effective:

(1) By deliberate destruction at the hands of the enemy.

As already stated Termonde is only one of a great number of towns and villages which have been similarly destroyed.

(2) By destruction done by the Belgians themselves to protect certain places.

Antwerp is a typical example. Everything that could afford cover to the enemy had been destroyed. Along the line which the enemy was expected to follow in his advance it had been found necessary to destroy several villages. In addition, a great tract of country had been flooded, and presented the appearance of a huge inland sea. The illusion would have been complete had it not been for the tops of hedges and high banks rising here and there above the surface of the water.

(3) By the enemy's bombardment.

The damage from this cause has been of a most devastating character. The most typical examples are Liège, Namur, Malines, Aerschot. But there are many more. The German siege guns have been the revelation of the war. At a range of seven miles they drop an enormously heavy shell. This usually

The Harvest
(HET KOREN IS RIJP)

destroys entirely any building that it hits, and starts great fires.

Sometimes a town has suffered bombardment, and afterwards has been wholly or partially destroyed after occupation by the enemy. A portion of Liège suffered this fate, as also did Louvain.

(4) By the arrest of the national life.

Possibly this is the most serious of all the forms of destruction which Belgium has suffered. The ordinary life of the people is at an end. Numbers which run into millions are refugees in foreign lands. Whole cities, like Antwerp, are practically empty. No trade or commerce is carried on. The factories are silent, the many coal mines are deserted, the shops are closed. Most serious of all, perhaps, agriculture is at a standstill. The peasants have fled from the fields, the crops are trampled by the contending armies.

The National Government has had to fly to France. The postal and telegraphic services are suspended, and all the amenities which a nation builds up in the course of the centuries.

So far I have written only of material damage. I have not spoken of the loss of the greatest of all treasure—human life. To the loss inseparable from the arbitrament of war there must be added in this case the great numbers of women and young people who have perished from exposure and famine as they fled from their homes and the civilians of all classes who met their death at the hands of the enemy.

The civilians have suffered most heavily of all.

Their homes and property have been destroyed Their leaders, spiritual and secular, have not infrequently been executed. In the rush from the stricken cities children have often been separated from their parents and lost. The aged and the sick have in many cases perished during the flight. So, too, have many children.

The sufferings of the Belgian wounded soldiers must be imagined. Antwerp served as the general hospital base for the whole of Belgium. The schools, colleges, and public buildings were converted into temporary hospitals. When the bombardment of Antwerp began it was decided to remove all these wounded. They were put into motor-buses and every conceivable kind of vehicle. The removal took place under shell fire. Buildings were ablaze in all directions. The wounded joined that great exodus. After indescribable sufferings, to which many of them succumbed on the journey, they reached Ghent, only to be immediately sent on to Ostend, for Ghent was unsafe. These are things that do not bear thinking of.

THE FUTURE

What does the future hold for Belgium?

I write on the assumption that the country will be restored to her people. But what will be her condition? Many of her towns and villages are wholly destroyed. Before they could be rebuilt the existing ruins must be carted away. The bulk of

The Exodus

(WAAR ZOU VADER LIGGEN?)

her people have fled to other lands. All the activities of a nation have ceased. No factories are working, no trade is done. Agriculture is at an end. The peasants have fled from their fields and farms. The troops have trampled the harvest. All is desolation and decay. And great as the ruin is at the moment, it grows worse day by day.

But there is another side to this black picture. It is not easy to kill a nation. It is like trying to kill thought. At the end of Shorthouse's wonderful romance, Mr Inglesant watches in the setting sun 'a glorious city, bathed in life and hope, full of happy people who thronged its streets and bridge, and the margin of its gentle stream. Then the sunset faded, and the ethereal vision vanished, and the landscape lay dark and chill.

'The sun is set...but it will rise again.'

So it is with Belgium. Her people will rise once more. They will rebuild their cities. They will recreate their homes. They will re-establish their commerce. They will become once more the nation they were.

But these things are not yet. Belgium is now in the hour of her need. She wants our help and it must be given in overwhelming measure. But we are not helping a nation which is going to perish. She will emerge again.

The spirit of the nation may be seen in the spirit of her King. Let me offer this tribute, however inadequate, to the courage, the genius, and the splendid heroism of the King of the Belgians. The manner in which he has faced unexampled misfortunes has revealed his character to the world. Known as one of the most modest and gentle of men, his conduct in this crisis has revealed a great statesman and a great leader. In part this has been a revelation even to the Belgians themselves, and has been the inspiring factor in the national action.

STEPS FOR THE BRITISH GOVERNMENT

In conclusion, there are two steps which I think the Government might take for the assistance of Belgium apart from their schemes for the refugees in this country. The first is to send a Commission to Holland to co-operate with representatives of neutral countries in getting food supplies and other necessaries of life to the non-combatants. The Government should place at the disposal of this Commission whatever food supplies are necessary.

The second is to establish the machinery for the help of the Belgian Government when it becomes possible for them and their people to return. It is then that our help will be most needed. It may well prove indispensable. For if the army which has invaded Belgium were to leave the country for ever to-day, it would be impossible for the Belgians to resume possession of their land immediately. The details given in this book supply the reasons. The life of the nation as a whole has been for the time being ruined. Whole cities and towns have been entirely destroyed. It is, therefore, a physical impossibility for the Belgians to return to their homes in many thousands of cases. It will be necessary to cart away the *débris* of whole cities before any attempt can be made to build new homes for the former citizens. It cannot be done in a day. Nor can the arrested life of a nation be quickly resumed. It can only resume its normal channel slowly.

When the Belgians return to their country they have to begin, so to speak, at the beginning again. Houses, churches, factories have to be built. Furniture has to be made. Machinery must be replaced. Farming operations have to be reorganised. The trades and manufactures of the nation have to be restarted.

How can we help in this renascence? Let us offer the Belgian nation, through a properly qualified Commission set up by the Government, the services of our own experts in the various departments of industry and art which have to be reconstituted in Belgium. She will want the guidance and help of builders, of architects, of manufacturers, of agriculturists, of experts in every department of national activity. What I am suggesting is really the setting up of a national clearing-house, where the representatives of every profession and trade here who desire to give any kind of help to Belgium in the day when it is possible to begin the rebuilding of her national life may bring their offers of service, however diverse the forms of the service may be, and have such offers co-ordinated, and the help they stand for organised, in a scientific manner, by an official body which would act in co-operation with the Belgian Government. We can give guidance and help in overflowing measure, and in doing so we shall assist Belgium once more to emerge from this sorrow and find her rightful place again.

> Who is this that rises with wounds so splendid;
>   All her brow and breast made beautiful with scars,
> In her eyes a light as of long pain ended,
>   In her mouth a song as of the morning stars?

www.ingramcontent.com/pod-product-compliance
Ingram Content Group UK Ltd.
Pitfield, Milton Keynes, MK11 3LW, UK
UKHW042150280225
455719UK00001B/230